TAYLOR TRADE PUBLISHING

Lanham • New York • Boulder • Toronto • Plymouth, UK

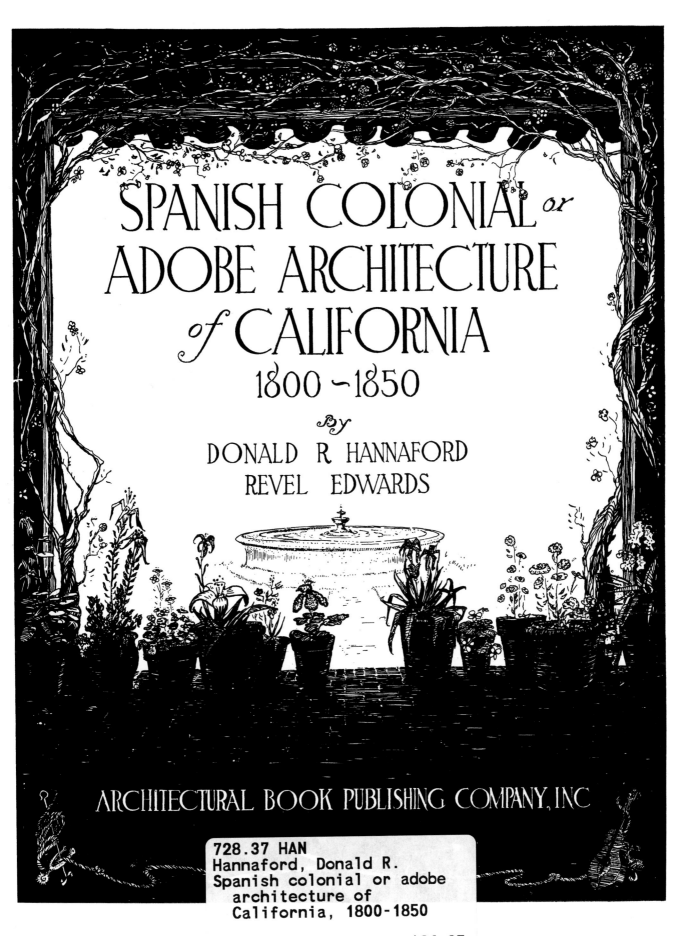

SPANISH COLONIAL or ADOBE ARCHITECTURE of CALIFORNIA
1800 ~ 1850

By

DONALD R. HANNAFORD
REVEL EDWARDS

ARCHITECTURAL BOOK PUBLISHING COMPANY, INC

Architectural Book Publishing Company
Published by Taylor Trade Publishing
An imprint of The Rowman & Littlefield Publishing Group, Inc.
4501 Forbes Boulevard, Suite 200, Lanham, Maryland 20706
www.rowman.com

Estover Road, Plymouth PL6 7PY, United Kingdom

Distributed by National Book Network

The cloth edition of this book was previously catalogued by the Library of
Congress. Catalog Card Number: 89-6516

ISBN 978-1-58979-684-3 (pbk. : alk. paper)
ISBN 978-1-58979-685-0 (electronic)

∞™ The paper used in this publication meets the minimum requirements
of American National Standard for Information Sciences—Permanence of
Paper for Printed Library Materials, ANSI/NISO Z39.48-1992.

Printed in the United States of America

FOREWORD

ABOUT four years ago, two harassed draftsmen, searching for a book, or at least a little authentic information concerning the adobe or Monterey type of house, finally decided in despair that any printed material on the subject would have to be collected by themselves.

Subsequently, in making our studies of these old houses, we found them highly interesting as an indigenous architecture of distinctive appeal. The remaining examples were being rapidly destroyed or unmercifully "restored" and the survivors of the old families fast disappearing. The great migration to the west, of the last thirty years, and the over-imaginative zeal of enthusiastic Californians from Iowa had done much to spoil the simple dignity of this period of California.

To architects, artists, historians, and others, a first hand knowledge—carefully prepared measured drawings, photographs, and sketches more accurate than artistic—was badly needed, and only a book could properly contain this wealth of material.

While one of us studied the two districts that most strongly influenced this architecture—tramping through the New England states for a year or so making notes and sketches; then wandering about southern Spain with the guitanos and carteros, occasionally working in the little brick and tile yards absorbing the native traditions of building (and the excellent wines)—the other was prowling about dark alleys and other likely hiding places of adobes, searching maps, historical records, deeds, and even personal letters, not to mention listening to the reminiscences of "old timers." Friends, seeing the far away look in his eye, thought he was either in love or contemplating murder. However, in a few years most of the adobes were located; some were covered with boarding or stucco, others were entirely surrounded by modern buildings, but by this time he could sense an adobe in any condition.

The preliminary work done, we traveled together many thousands of miles over country roads of the state, making measured drawings, sketches, and photographs. Through the kindness of Mr. L. S. Slevins, of Carmel, who permitted us to use eight of his early photographs of some of the houses now destroyed or restored beyond recognition, we have a complete record of this period of "native" architecture—except those too small to be of architectural value.

We are most indebted to Mr. Elmer C. Richardson through whose encouragement and generosity the book was made possible. To the descendants of the old families of California—to Mr. and Mrs. Serrano, Mrs. Gragg, Mrs. Toolman, and Mrs. Powers, of Monterey —Mr. Adler of Sonoma—Mr. Fleischman of Santa Barbara, and to the host of others who courteously opened their homes to us for photographing and measuring; we wish to express our sincere appreciation and thanks.

D. R. H.
Monterey, January, 1931

PREFACE

By David Gebhard

BY the time Donald Hannaford and Revel Edwards produced this volume California had enjoyed some thirty years of romantic play with its Hispanic architectural inheritance. In the early 1890s, the image of the Mission churches had formed the bases for the regionalism of the famed Mission Revival. In the early nineteen hundreds, the Mission image had been joined by Italian Mediterranean country houses and gardens.[1] Eventually, in the teens, the Mission and Mediterranean modes gave way to a passionate involvement with the Spanish Colonial Revival which held the center of the stage through much of the 1920s.[2]

Though the early writers on California's Hispanic tradition—Helen Hunt Jackson, Charles F. Lummis and George Wharton James—had all discussed the adobe dwellings of Alta California, these "native" buildings had surprisingly not served as an influential design source for any of California's Hispanic revivals. As Donald Hannaford remarked in his Foreword, the interest in the California adobe came about because of a shift in predilection which brought to the fore other Hispanic episodes, particularly that of the Monterey and California Ranch House. The revival of the Monterey and California Ranch House was perceived as having a decided advantage over any of the earlier affairs, for a modern interpretation of a balconied Monterey house, or of a low spreading California ranch house related directly to actual historic types; and they could at the same time pertain to the national Anglo Colonial Revival image.

The interest of architects in the adobes of California commenced in the early 1890s. Ernest Coxhead and Willis Polk sketched many of the state's principal adobes, reaching from Los Angeles to Monterey. By the mid 1890s, other practitioners—Samuel Newsom, Arthur B. Benton and Sumner Hunt—had not only sketched many of the existing adobes, but they had written about them as well and argued for their preservation along with the mission churches. The romanticized image of California's nineteenth century adobes entered into the turn of the century Craftsman movement, but only in a selective way via patios, columned corridors, stucco walls and tile roofs.

Along with the Mission churches many of the existing historic adobes of California were restored and re-restored in the years after 1900. These restorations were not based upon any historic studies of the state's adobe tradition, rather they mirrored a wonderfully imaginative and romantic view of what life was like (or perhaps as a mythical ideal should have been like) in early nineteenth century California.

[1]Karen J. Weitz, *California's Mission Revival* (Santa Monica: Hennesey and Ingalls, 1984); David Gebhard, "Architectural Imagery, The Missions and California," *The Harvard Architectural Review* 1 (Spring, 1984): 137–145.

[2]David Gebhard, *George Washington Smith, The Spanish Colonial Revival in California* (Santa Barbara: University of California, 1964).

The first individual on the scene who made a systematic effort to record some of the adobes via measured drawings was the architect, Rexford Newcomb. The result of his studies of the Mission Churches and of the adobes was published in a series of articles during the years 1919 through 1921 in the pages of *The Western Architect*. In 1925 Newcomb gathered these articles together and published them in a single volume, *The Old Mission Churches and Historic Houses of California*.

By 1931, when Hannaford and Edwards published their volume, there was a scattering of articles on the adobes of California, most of which found their way into the pages of the popular home magazines—ranging from *Sunset Magazine* and *California Arts and Architecture*, to *House and Garden*, *House Beautiful*, and *Country Life*. Almost exclusively, the subject of these articles was the Anglo/Hispanic Monterey style, not the pre-1830 Spanish and Mexican adobes. The intent of the authors of these articles was to construct a convincing historic tale which could serve as a basis for the then emerging revival of the Monterey style.[3]

While the illustrations of photographs and the text of these articles obviously provided inspiration for clients and architects, what was missing was a wide array of photographs of these adobes, and above all there was a lack of measured drawings. In contrast, an architect working within the Colonial Revival, or the French Norman and English Tudor was, by 1930, provided with numerous books and articles presenting photographs, and above all measured drawings of details of these historic styles.

Thus for practicing architects, Hannaford and Edwards' volume became the main published source, and remains so today, of photographs and drawings of the early adobes. Beginning in the early thirties, the Historic American Building Survey started its recording of many of California's historic adobes.[4] While a few of these H.A.B.S. drawings and photographs were published, most were not. In the years immediately after World War II several books were published which did provide drawings and photographs of the early adobes. Certainly the most useful of these was Cliff May's *Sunset Western Ranch Houses* of 1946; Clarence Cullimore's *Santa Barbara Adobes* of 1948; and Helen I. Griffen's *Casa and Courtyards: Historic Houses of California* of 1955. Still, not withstanding the great popularity of the California Ranch house image during these years, none of these newer publications equaled in completeness the array of adobes presented by Hannaford and Edwards, nor did any of these publications of the Post War II years contain the measured drawings of details presented by these authors.

A final observation should be made relating to the condition of the adobes as they were photographed and drawn by the authors. As Hannaford's text illustrates they were well aware of the fact that the adobes, as they were experiencing them in the 1920s, were highly altered buildings: structures which had been modified, added to and changed over the years. As with early H.A.B.S

---

[3]Knowlton Mixer, "The Monterey House," *House Beautiful* 71 (February 1933): 49–51; Roland E. Coate, "The Early California House," *California Arts and Architecture* 35 (March 1929): 21–30; Archie T. Newsom, "Style: California Colonial," *The Architect and Engineer* 123 (October 1935): 11–27; David Gebhard, "The Monterey Tradition: History Reordered," *New Mexico Studies in Fine Arts* 7 (1982): 14–19.

[4]"Historic American Building Survey: Early California Houses of Varying Types and Materials," *The Architect and Engineer* 120 (March 1935): 31–37; Sally B. Woodbridge, *California Architecture: Historic American Building Survey* (San Francisco: Chronicle Books, 1988).

program of the 1930s Hannaford and Edwards accepted the buildings as they found them, and they made no effort (as for example Clarence Cullimore did in his 1947 volume) to suggest any reconstruction of what the adobes might have looked like when they were initially built, and how they may have been modified over the years. Neither did they engage in any historical research to assertain when each of these adobes was in fact built. Their declared task was to furnish clients and architects with visual documentation of existing adobe buildings which could serve as points of departure for the continual revivals of California's early nineteenth century Hispanic and Anglo past. In this self assigned mission they succeeded admirably.

INTRODUCTION

THE architecture of the Missions, which has been the subject of much research, lies in a category by itself and owes much to the foreign influences brought by the padres from their native lands and to the thousands of Indian workmen who executed their designs. It is therefore to the smaller adobes we must look to find work conceived first by the Spanish Dons to meet their simple needs of living, and, later, that type of architecture developed from the intermingling of traditional ideas of the New England pioneers with the Spanish and their consequent adaptations with the building materials at hand.

During the years between 1830 and 1840, the country was very prosperous. Monterey, a sea port and the capitol of California at that time, was the center of life in the northern part of the State for the big ranches of the interior. Hides and tallow were plentiful and trading with the East coast was at its height. It was only natural, then as always, that wealth gave the time for social and cultural activities, and the inevitable building that followed is in itself a transcript of history, showing the virtues and defects in the lives of those producing it.

The larger houses, and even the cottages, were built for comfort and convenience and each suits its location, showing more than anything else that what is best adapted for its purpose is the most beautiful. They never pretended to be anything but what they were; there seems to have been no effort to complicate their construction or ornamentation, but merely a simple handing-on from generation to generation, from both the New England and Spanish settlers, of well worn and tried traditions worked with the materials of the locality. There is, as a rule, nothing forced or fantastic in their outline nor frivolous in their detail—if there is picturesque confusion, it is the result of successive additions made with sympathetic materials and a directness of purpose, rather than of conscious effort.

The old adobes are not all beautiful or well built; time has softened many of the faults of those that have withstood earthquakes, progress, and the elements. Yet through them all runs that simplicity of design that comes from straightforward methods of solving problems of construction and the needs of those who dwelt therein.

The adobes of California possess many points in common—although those of the north, especially on the coast, were more influenced by workmen with New England traditions (many were ship carpenters)—and no attempt, therefore, is made to deal with them here from any novel standpoint or to trace at length their architectural or historical evolution, but merely to draw attention to some of the typical features, both in their design and construction, that developed a distinctive type of architecture.

Except in the towns—where the established streets to a certain extent dictated the orientation—the houses, as a rule, were placed crosswise to the points of the compass so the sun, at some time of day, would shine into every room. The patio or courtyard was used as much for living as the house, usually facing south with the veranda on the north side (of patio) so it would get the warmth of the sun all day during the winter months. In many cases the veranda extended around three sides of the patio and was used as a corridor for rooms that would otherwise have been inter-communicating.

In brief, the typical plan of the early house was well adapted to the simple and hospitable life of the times. On the ground floor was the living room, dining room, ball room (if any), kitchen and storage rooms, and the veranda from which stairs led up to the balcony. All bed rooms were usually on the second floor and entered off the balcony; they were also inter-communicating. Of course some of the houses, particularly those built for the Yankees, had inside stairs. But these were few. Later, however, practically all the outside stairs were removed and new ones built inside. It is now rare to find one on the exterior.

As the different types resembled each other in the relation of plan to elevation, so did they in their construction—which was simple in the extreme. Labor and dirt being plentiful, it was the natural thing to build, as the Mission builders had done, with sun dried adobe bricks. There was an abundance of redwood and pine in the forests but it was difficult to saw into lumber; then, too, the adobe walls kept the heat out in the summer and retained it in the winter. They also afforded better protection against stray bullets and Indian attacks, both of which there were many in the early days. In Monterey there is limestone, or "chalk rock" as it is called by the "natives," but only one house of the period was built entirely of this material.

It is doubtful if there ever existed any formula, other than the recommendations of one's neighbor, for the making of adobe bricks. From some of the direct descendants of the old Spanish families, we have gathered the few facts that follow. A large basin about twenty feet in diameter and two feet deep was dug in the ground near the building site; into this was put loam, sand, clay, and straw, tile chips or other binder; then the materials mixed with water to a thick soupy consistency; the mixture then taken out, put into molds, and dried in the sun. This seems to have been the best method, for it is now clear to see that the well made bricks have stood the ravages of time far better than those of loosely packed coarse aggregate.

The walls were laid on light foundations, if any, of stone; which accounts for the ever present seeping of dampness, and the falling of walls during severe earth shocks. If a concrete foundation were used—one strong enough to sustain the heavy weight of the walls—adobe would still be a most satisfactory material to use in most parts of California.

On the ground floor, walls average about three feet in thickness and on the upper, about two feet. The offset, as a rule, being on the inside to add greater floor space to the rooms. Occasionally, it was on the outside with a few buttresses, the full width of the lower wall, extending up to the roof—as on the front of the Castro house at San Juan. Walls were laid with, approximately one inch wide, mud mortar joints. Chips of tile or small bits of broken pottery were often mixed with the mortar to give added strength.

The walls of the better houses were covered with mud plaster, which, by the way, was remarkably smooth and even in texture; after this, they were heavily whitewashed at least once a year to protect the surface from rain. "The whitewasher's brush is never still" is an old Spanish proverb that was very true in California, for on many of the old walls the whitewash is so thick it really forms a hard coat of lime plaster. Many of the walls that were either not plastered in the beginning or from which it had fallen, were later refinished with lime plaster, often marked off to imitate stone.

The use of boarding as a wall covering was usually a later addition or a protection for a crumbling adobe wall. Both V-joint and board and batten siding are found, but both were used sparingly.

There is an idea afoot, as is shown by some of the present day imitators in their "copies," that the walls were bulgy and bumpy. This is seldom so; however, many of the walls were not straight. The Olivos ranch house, for instance, has an outward curve of about eighteen inches in the front wall, but it is a graceful sweep and is barely perceptible in the wall which is about fifty feet in length.

Roof coverings varied in different localities. Where redwood was abundant, hand riven shingles or shakes were used; and tile, where good clay was found. Many of the houses originally having shake or shingle roofs were later covered with tile; many that were of tile are now covered with shingles—due in many cases to the low financial conditions of the owners who, in later years, sold their tiles; but far too often to the ruthless pilaging of some well meaning citizen of a nearby town. But no matter now—whether of tile or shakes, the roofs are green with moss and either material is fitting.

The original tiles were hand made; some say over a shapely thigh, but this is highly improbable—it would have taken a small army of hardy legs to supply the thousands of human molds necessary to produce all the tiles used on these old buildings. The authors have seen many of the wooden molds over which tiles were shaped and believe that to have been the general method. To those who prefer to accept the first method—we would like to see the legs responsible for some of the tiles we have seen, for they were sixteen inches across the big end.

Roof textures will best be left to the reader's examination of the photographs. An odd, but practical, custom was to use shakes on the balcony roof and tile on the rest of the roof. The reason, of course, was to relieve the cantilevered balcony from the additional weight of the tile.

Chimneys, simple in design and usually small in size—due to fireplaces built for heating rather than ornamentation, were invariably built in inside walls; hence came through the roof rather than being on the exterior of the building. There are exceptions, of course.

Gable vents were rarely used, because the space between eaves plate and top of rafters was usually open and gave ample ventilation for the attic.

Balconies were of three distinct types. The first, and most common, with supporting posts from the ground to the roof; second, the cantilevered balcony with posts supporting the roof; and third, of which only one example remains, the cantilevered balcony and cantilevered roof with no supporting posts. Practically all balconies and verandas had closed ends of wide vertical boarding or simple lattice work which gave more privacy and partial protection from the wind. As the three types are clearly illustrated with measured drawings, further discussion here would be superfluous.

The massive walls seem to radiate a welcome; and to enter the venerable houses is to know again the sincere hospitality that once prevailed in California. It is the satisfying proportions of the rooms, rather than studied detail, that gives to them this friendly feeling.

The wide hand hewn pine planks of the second floor and the hewn joists that carry them, usually form the ceilings of the lower floor rooms. The walls are, in most houses, of white plaster—sometimes papered. In one aged room we counted fourteen layers and found one of newspapers bearing the date 1849.

Much of the refinement is due to the exquisitely proportioned double hung windows—feminine in their daintiness. Panes, Colonial in scale, average eight by ten inches in size. The muntins, details of which will be found at the back of the book, were never over one-half inch wide and more often only seven sixteenths. Windows were usually set flush with the outside of the wall; the deep reveal, splayed about ten inches on each side and often paneled, was on the inside, forming a sort of bay or window seat.

Shutters were sometimes on the inside, folding back against the reveal; sometimes on the outside; and occasionally shutter blinds outside and paneled shutters inside. In the Larkin house, the reveal is so paneled that when the shutter is folded back it becomes a part of the reveal paneling.

Exterior doors were often in pairs—each door being barely wide enough to pass through. On the inside, for protection in addition to the lock and bolts, a wooden bar—fitting into wrought iron brackets on each jamb—that could be placed across both doors, was frequently used. Interior doors were of varied designs and sizes—often five feet nine inches in height and generally not over six feet. Wrought or cast iron butt hinges of various types and sizes and, often, surface hinges of simple design were used on interior doors. Of the many large surface locks so commonly used in the early days, only a few remain. Through the years they have disappeared or have been replaced with modern locks; however, on almost every door can be seen a few marks or holes where the original lock was fastened.

Upper floor rooms, as a rule, had ceilings of wide pine boards with beaded joints. As wooden lath was difficult to obtain, plaster ceilings, were they occur, are often the result of later remodeling.

In some of the early adobes the lower floors were of tile, but with the advent of the Americans, came dancing; so in due time a more suitable wooden floor, raised about six inches above the level of adjoining rooms, was built in many a home, and the "sale" or ball room was created. This, in part, explains the difference of floor levels found in some of the houses.

Before closing, a brief comment on colors seems necessary. Exterior walls, eaves, rough woodwork, and under sides of balcony roofs, were commonly whitewashed—often a delicate pink, or a cream slightly off white. Balconies were frequently painted white, soft green, or warm gray, and sometimes whitewashed. Exterior doors, shutters, and trim were painted various tones of green, gray, or brown, and occasionally to match the walls.

Interior walls were invariably white. Ceilings sometimes painted light olive green, dull white, or warm gray; and not infrequently blue or whitewashed. Woodwork was white, deep cream, or gray green. Mantles were sometimes white, cream, or gray, but most often dull black; which after all was a very sensible color for them. In short: Color was the result of the dictates of fancy rather than of tradition.

Picket fences and adobe garden walls are prominent characteristic features. They are the ties between house and garden—the last elementary touch that completes and blends the two into a harmonious ensemble.

The destruction of ancient houses and their associations is a serious matter in any country, even after thoughtful consideration with what to replace them. It is unpardonable that our architectural heritage—so closely interwoven with the life and history of the country—is rapidly being swept away to make room for what, in most cases, can only be regarded as doubtful improvement.

Go where we will amongst these old adobe houses: contemplate any that have been untouched by the hand of the restorer and it is impossible not to be impressed by their beauty and subtle charm. The aged walls covered with moss and the discolorations of time, the absence of needless ornament, and the feeling of homeliness that pervades every feature, all combine to produce this simple and beautiful architecture.

Donald R. Hannaford

VALLEJO HOUSE - MONTEREY

LARKIN HOUSE, MONTEREY

LARKIN HOUSE AT MONTEREY

LARKIN HOUSE AT MONTEREY

LARKIN HOUSE, MONTEREY

FRONT ENTRANCE

ESCOLLES HOUSE MONTEREY

ESCOLLES HOUSE, MONTEREY

REAR LOGGIA, ESCOLLES HOUSE, MONTEREY

KITCHEN WING OF THE ESCOLLES HOUSE, MONTEREY

7

BALCONY DETAILS, ESCOLLES HOUSE, MONTEREY

8

BALCONY

THE ESCOLLES HOUSE, MONTEREY

PICKET FENCE

9

VERANDA

THE SOBERANES HOUSE, MONTEREY

BALCONY

The Soberanes House, Monterey

Gable

LIMESTONE HOUSE MONTFREY

OLD WHALING STATION, MONTEREY

14

East End

Front Entrance

THE OLD WHALING STATION, MONTEREY

15

SHERMAN ROSE COTTAGE AT MONTEREY

ENTRANCE GATES TO SHERMAN ROSE COTTAGE, MONTEREY

OLD ADOBE MONTEREY
(Covered with boarding)

OVEN

HOUSE AT MONTEREY

GENERAL SHERMAN'S HEADQUARTERS, MONTEREY

DOOR DETAIL, SHERMAN HEADQUARTERS, MONTEREY

GATE TO PATIO, SHERMAN ROSE COTTAGE, MONTEREY

WINDOW DETAIL AT MONTEREY

COTTAGE AT MONTEREY

HOUSE AT MONTEREY

GENERAL SHERMAN'S HEADQUARTERS, MONTEREY

COTTAGE MONTEREY

McKINLEY HOUSE, MONTEREY

McKinley House, Monterey

Balcony Detail

23

McKinley House, Monterey

Window Grille

24

GARDEN GATE, LARKIN HOUSE, MONTEREY

COURTYARD GATES, McKINLEY HOUSE

FRONT ENTRANCE, JOSE CASTRO HOUSE, SAN JUAN

ONE OF THE FIRST HOUSES BUILT OF MILLED LUMBER, MONTEREY

CASTRO HOUSE SAN JUAN

CASTRO HOUSE, SAN JUAN

Balcony

28

JOSE CASTRO HOUSE AT SAN JUAN

CUSTOM HOUSE FROM THE BAY OF MONTEREY

29

CUSTOM HOUSE AT MONTEREY

CUSTOM HOUSE AT MONTEREY

UNA CASA CERCA DE SAN JUAN

THE STEVENSON HOUSE, REAR VIEW, MONTEREY

THE SERRANO HOUSE AT MONTEREY

COURTYARD WASHINGTON HOTEL

PACIFIC BUILDING, MONTEREY, BUILT FOR A HOTEL

STEVENSON HOUSE AT MONTEREY

WASHINGTON HOTEL AT MONTEREY

THE OLD CALEDONIAN INN, NEAR SAN MIGUEL

COTTAGE AT MONTEREY

35

ENTRANCE GATES TO A COURTYARD, MONTEREY

ADOBE WALL, MONTEREY

OUTSIDE STAIR
MONTEREY

SHOP DOOR
MONTEREY

RECESSED WINDOW & DOOR
SAN JUAN.

ABREGO HOUSE AT MONTEREY

GABLE OF ABREGO HOUSE AT MONTEREY

The Abrego House, Monterey

Veranda Detail

39

DETAIL.

THE ABREGO HOUSE, MONTEREY

PATIO GATE

THE ABREGO HOUSE, MONTEREY

VIEW FROM PATIO

A GARDEN GATE IN MONTEREY

ADOBE WALL, MONTEREY

VERANDA AND ENTRANCE TO SMALL ADOBE, MONTEREY

GARDEN WALL OF THE LARKIN HOUSE, MONTEREY

GOVERNOR CASTROS HEADQUARTERS, MONTEREY

ADOBE BUILDING, MONTEREY

ADOBE OF THE BANDIT TIBURCIO VASQUEZ, MONTEREY

ADOBE COTTAGE AT MONTEREY

HEADQUARTERS OF FIRST SPANISH GOVERNOR OF CALIFORNIA, MONTEREY

DETAIL OF THE VERANDA

ADOBE HOUSE AT SONOMA

ADOBE AT PLEASANTON

HACIENDA HOUSE, VIEW FROM WEST BALCONY

VALLEJO HOUSE, FRONT VIEW, SONOMA

THE VALLEJO HACIENDA NEAR SONOMA

VALLEJO HOUSE, REAR VIEW, SONOMA

WINDOW DETAIL, PLEASANTON

ADOBE NEAR SALINAS

PART OF OLD "EL DORADO," SONOMA

THE BLUE WING TAVERN AT SONOMA

BLUE WING TAVERN · SONOMA

BLUE WING TAVERN AT SONOMA

ADLER ADOBE AT SONOMA

HOUSE NEAR SAN JUAN

ADOBE COTTAGE AT SANTA CLARA

ENTRANCE TO COURTYARD OF A RANCH, ALISAL DISTRICT

VACQUEROS QUARTERS, RANCH IN ALISAL DISTRICT

COURTYARD OF A RANCH, ALISAL DISTRICT, NEAR SALINAS

BALCONY OF ADOBE AT SAN JUAN

RANCH IN THE ALISAL DISTRICT, NEAR SALINAS

ADOBE IN THE CIENEGA VALLEY

CASTRO RANCH HOUSE NEAR SALINAS

HARTNELL COLLEGE, NEAR SALINAS

DE SOTO HOUSE, MONTEREY

RIO RANCH HOUSE, SAN MIGUEL

BUILDING AT SAN LOUIS OBISPO

THE BERENDO RANCH, NEAR SALINAS

VERANDA DETAIL, BERENDO HOUSE

RANCH HOUSE NEAR SANTA BARBARA

VERANDA OF RANCH HOUSE, NEAR SANTA BARBARA

PATIO OF DE LA GUERRA HOUSE, SANTA BARBARA

GARDEN WALL OF DE LA GUERRA HOUSE

THE ORENA HOUSE, REAR VIEW

THE ORENA HOUSE, SANTA BARBARA

OLD BARRACKS AT SANTA BARBARA

ENTRANCE ON ANACAPA STREET, SANTA BARBARA

GABLE DETAIL OF A SMALL ADOBE, SAN FERNANDO

COTTAGE AT SAN GABRIEL

THE ORTEGA HOUSE, FRONT VIEW, NEAR MONTECITO

THE ORTEGA HOUSE, REAR VIEW, NEAR MONTECITO

ADOBE AT SANTA CLARA

ADOBE AT SANTA BARBARA, ON SITE OF OLD PRESIDIO

THE OLIVOS RANCH HOUSE FROM THE PATIO, VENTURA

THE OLIVOS RANCH, FRONT VIEW

THE OLIVOS RANCH, NEAR VENTURA

THE OLIVOS RANCH HOUSE, FROM THE WEST

HOUSE AT SANTA BARBARA

CAMULOS RANCH HOUSE, NEAR PIRU

THE AVILA HOUSE, OLIVERA STREET, LOS ANGELES

UNA HUERTA DE SAN GABRIEL

OLIVERA STREET, PLAZA, LOS ANGELES

HOUSE ON OLIVERA STREET, LOS ANGELES

MEXICAN STORE - LOS ANGELES

THE LUGO HACIENDA, REAR VIEW, EAST LOS ANGELES

THE LUGO HACIENDA, FRONT VIEW

EL RANCHITO - DE DON PIO PICO

ESTUDILLO HOUSE, OLD TOWN, SAN DIEGO

DOORWAY, ESTUDILLO HOUSE, OLD TOWN, SAN DIEGO

WINDOW DETAIL, ESTUDILLO HOUSE, SAN DIEGO

RANCH HOUSE NEAR LONG BEACH

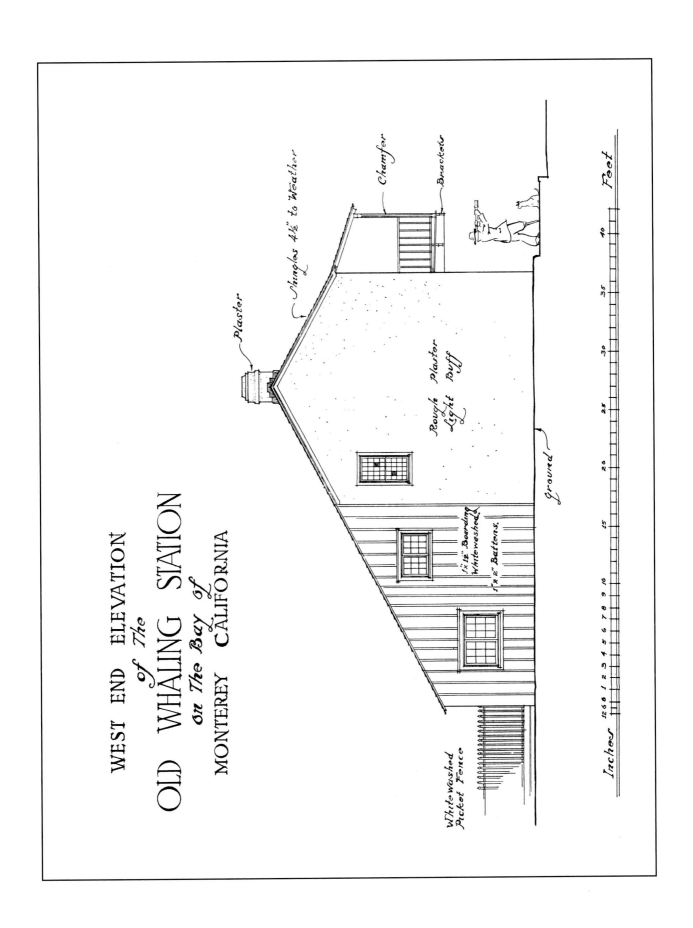

WEST END ELEVATION
of The
OLD WHALING STATION
on The Bay of
MONTEREY CALIFORNIA

Plaster

Shingles 4½" to Weather

Chamfer

Brackets

Rough Plaster
Light Buff

Ground

1"x12" Boarding
Whitewashed

1"x2" Battens

Whitewashed
Picket Fence

Inches 12 6 0 1 2 3 4 5 6 7 8 9 10   15   20   25   30   35   40   Feet

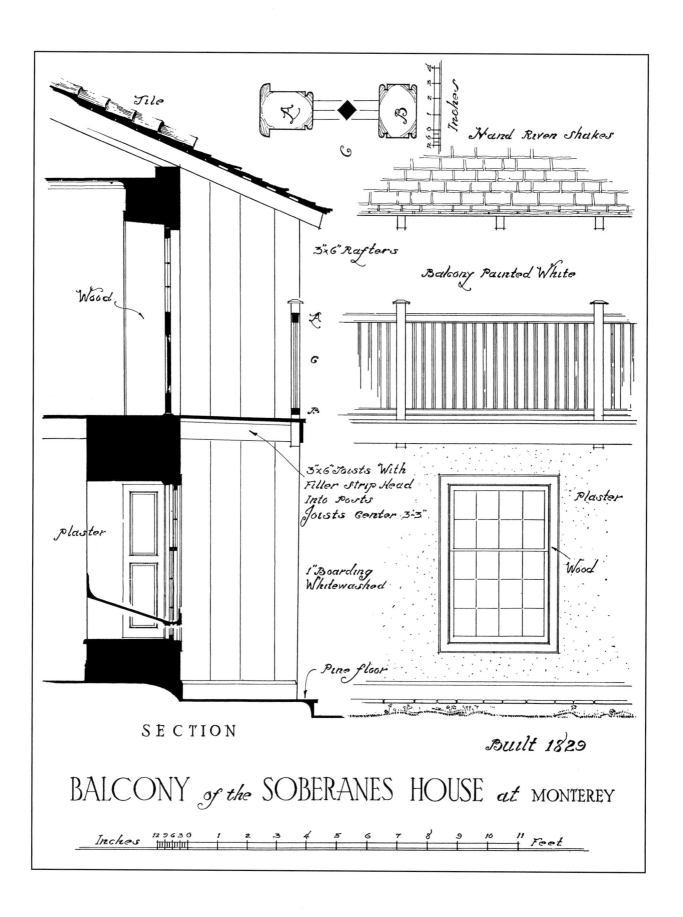

Tile

Hand Riven Shakes

Inches

Wood

3"x6" Rafters

Balcony Painted White

A

C

B

Plaster

3"x6" Joists With
Filler Strip Head
Into Posts
Joists Center 3'-3"

Plaster

1" Boarding
Whitewashed

Wood

Pine floor

SECTION

Built 1829

BALCONY *of the* SOBERANES HOUSE *at* MONTEREY

Inches   12 9 6 3 0   1   2   3   4   5   6   7   8   9   10   11   Feet

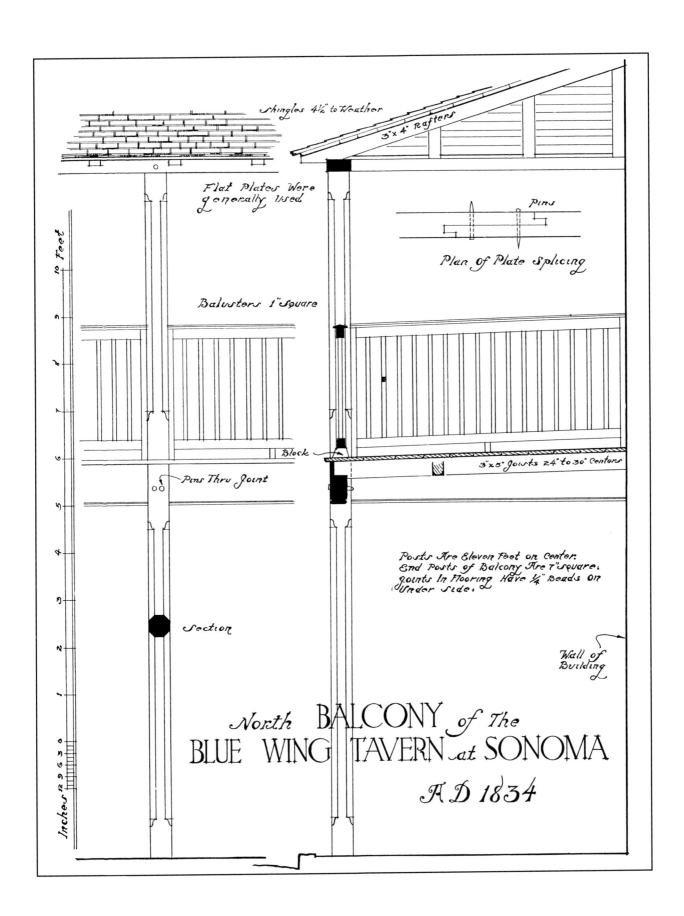

Shingles 4½" to Weather

3"x 4" Rafters

Flat Plates Were
generally Used

Pins

Plan of Plate Splicing

Balusters 1" Square

10 Feet

Block

Pins Thru Joint

3"x 5" Joists 24" to 30" Centers

Posts Are Eleven Feet on Center.
End Posts of Balcony Are 7" Square.
Joints In Flooring Have ¼" Beads On
Under Side.

Section

Wall of
Building

Inches

North BALCONY of The
BLUE WING TAVERN at SONOMA
AD 1834

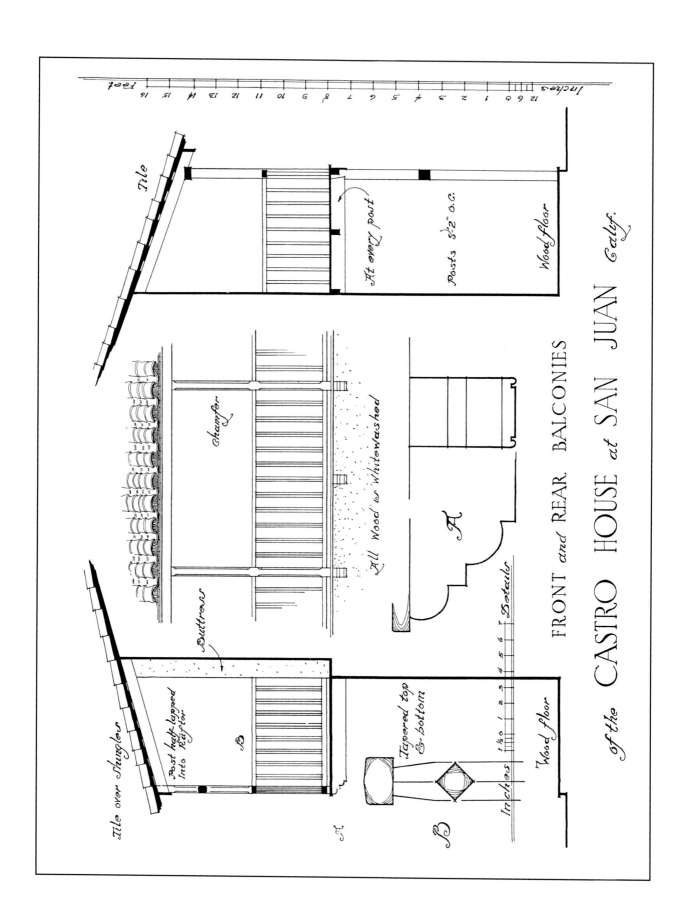

FRONT and REAR BALCONIES at SAN JUAN Calif.
of the CASTRO HOUSE

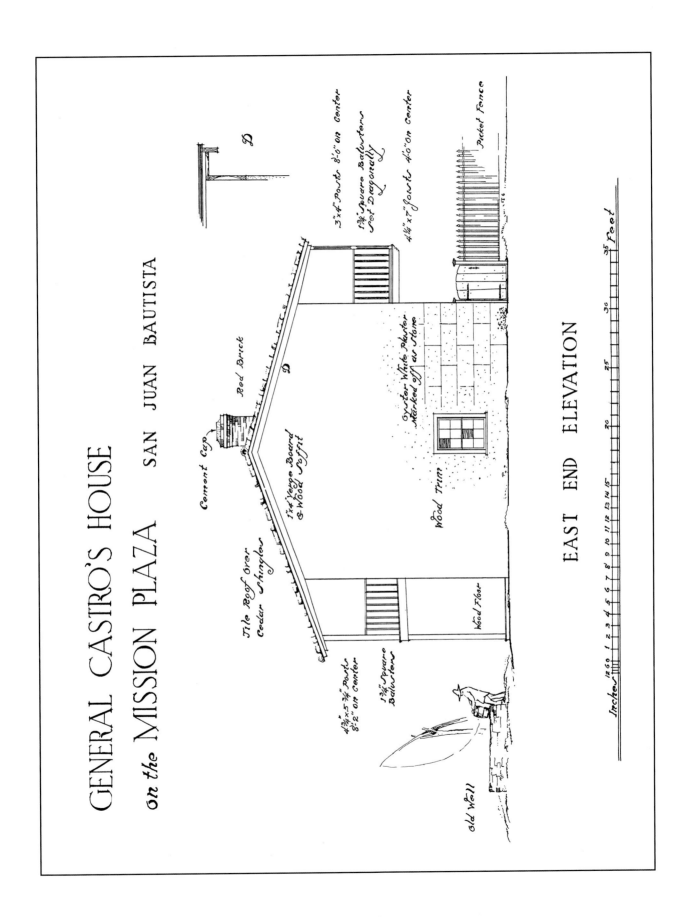

GENERAL CASTRO'S HOUSE   SAN JUAN BAUTISTA

on the MISSION PLAZA

EAST END ELEVATION

Tile Roof over Cedar Shingles

Cement Cap

Red Brick

1"x4" Verge Board & Wood Soffit

4¾" x 5¾" Posts 8'-2" on Center

1¾" Square Balusters

Wood Floor

old Well

Oyster White Plaster Marked off as Stone

Wood Trim

3"x4" Posts 8'-0" on Center

1¾" Square Balusters Set Diagonally

4¼"x7" Joists 4'-0" on Center

Picket Fence

Inches 12 6 0   1 2 3 4 5 6 7 8 9 10 11 12 13 14 15   20   25   30   35 Feet

89

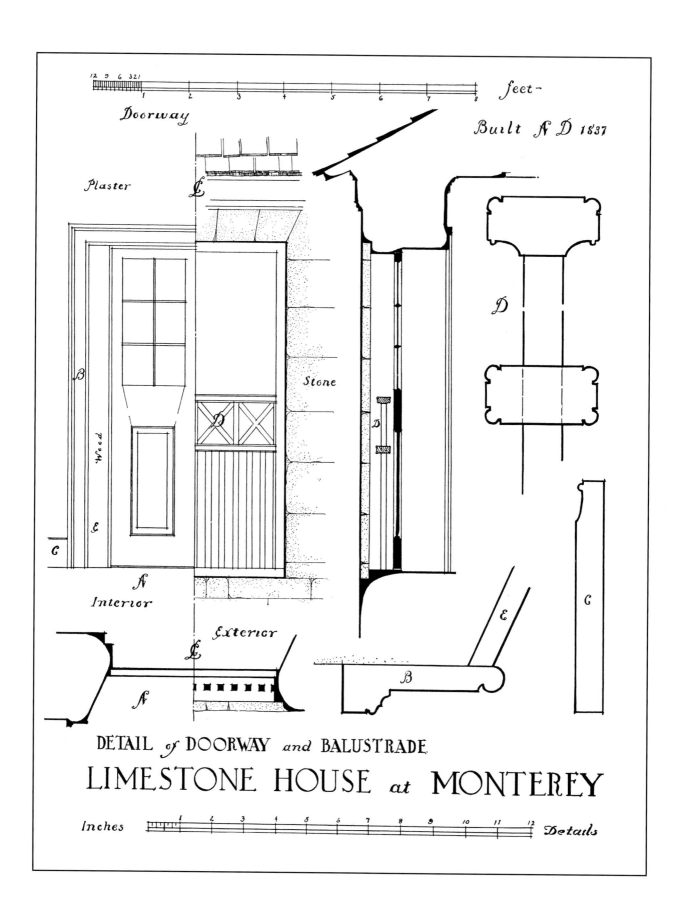

DETAIL of DOORWAY and BALUSTRADE.
LIMESTONE HOUSE at MONTEREY

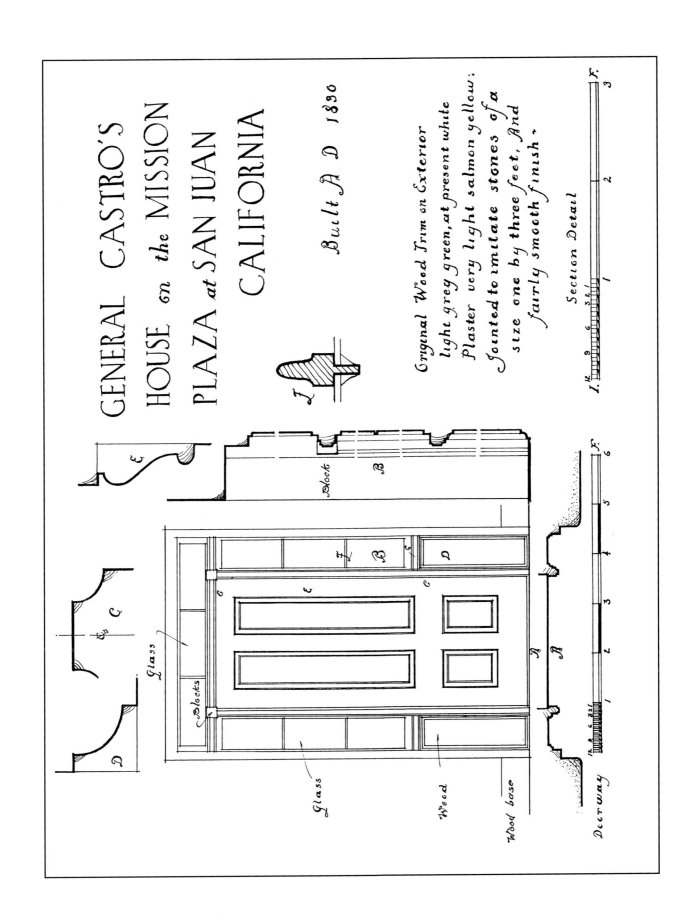

GENERAL CASTRO'S HOUSE on the MISSION PLAZA at SAN JUAN CALIFORNIA

Built A D 1830

Original Wood Trim on Exterior light grey green, at present white Plaster very light salmon yellow; Jointed to imitate stones of a size one by three feet, And fairly smooth finish.

Section Detail

Block

B

Glass

Blocks

Glass

Wood

Wood base

Doorway

Pilaster Cap

HOUSE on CARRILLO St.
SANTA BARBARA

Light Cadmium Yellow Plaster
Woodwork Light Olive Green
Rafters Light Cream Wash

TWO DOORWAYS

the ESCOLLES HOUSE
MONTEREY

Rough Texture Oyster White Plaster
Doors & Reveal Medium Burnt Umber
Porch Floor Gray Green

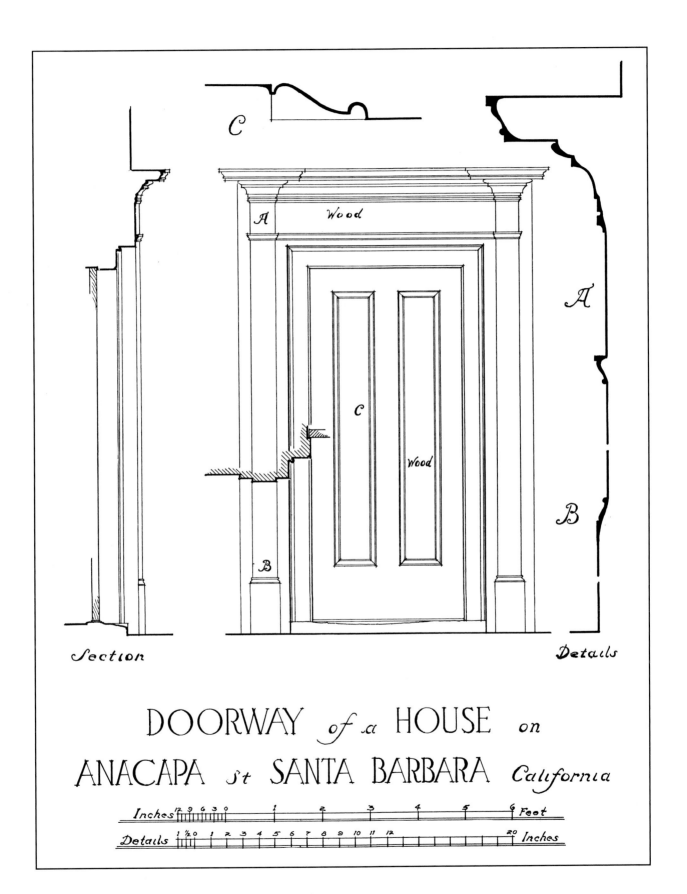

C

A   Wood

C

Wood

B

A

B

Section

Details

DOORWAY of a HOUSE on
ANACAPA St SANTA BARBARA California

Inches 12 9 6 3 0   1   2   3   4   5   6 Feet

Details 1½ 20   1 2 3 4 5 6 7 8 9 10 11 12   20 Inches

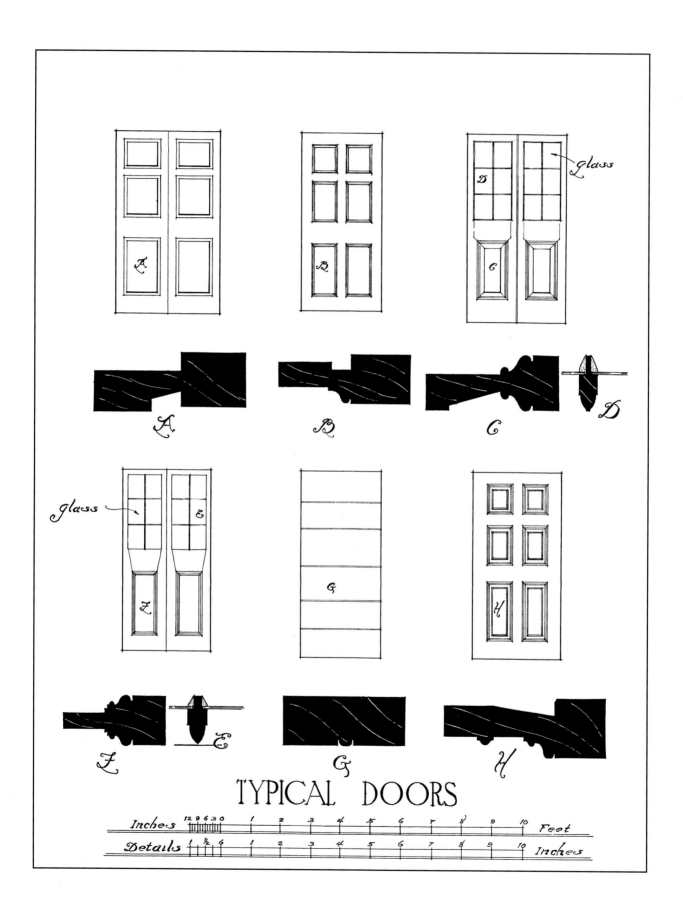

TYPICAL DOORS

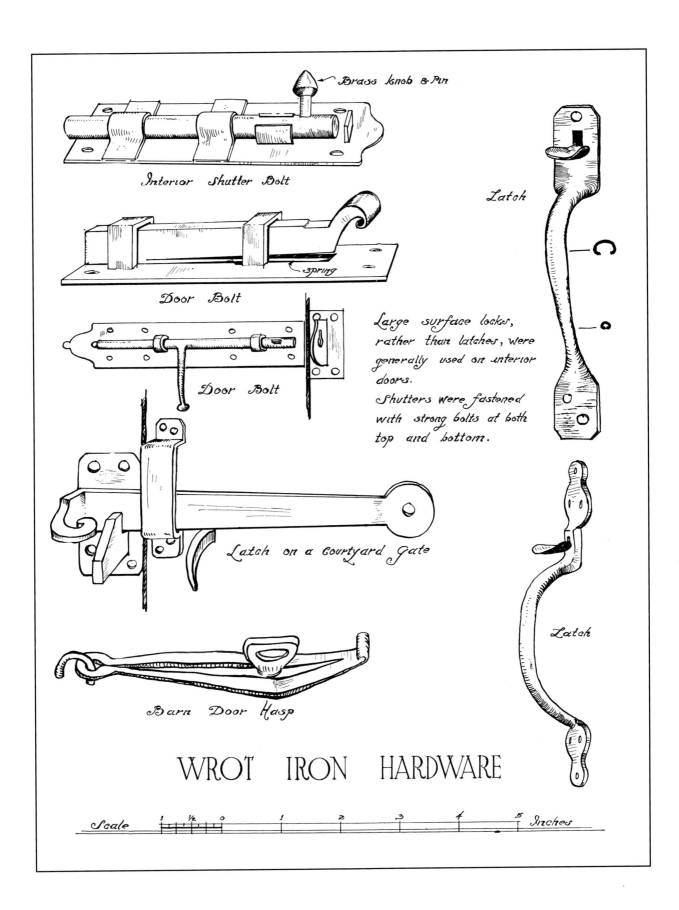

Brass Knob & Pin

Interior Shutter Bolt

Door Bolt

spring

Door Bolt

Latch on a Courtyard Gate

Barn Door Hasp

Latch

Large surface locks, rather than latches, were generally used on interior doors.
Shutters were fastened with strong bolts at both top and bottom.

Latch

WROT IRON HARDWARE

Scale   1   ½   0   1   2   3   4   5   Inches

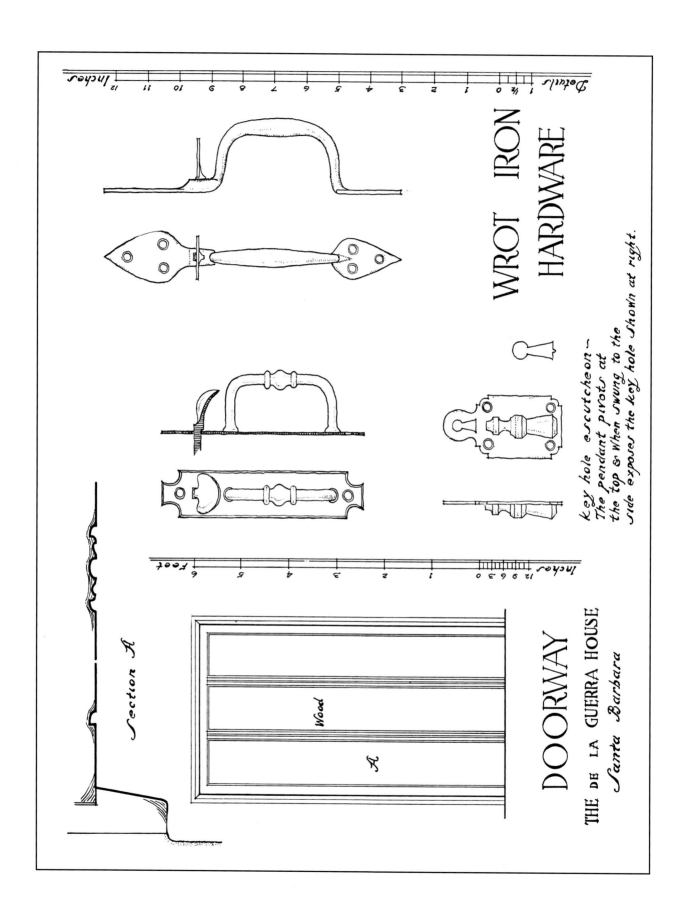

WROT IRON
HARDWARE

key hole escutcheon ~
The pendant pivots at
the top & when swung to the
side exposes the key hole shown at right.

DOORWAY

THE DE LA GUERRA HOUSE
Santa Barbara

Wood

A

Section A

Details   Inches
1 1/2 0 1 2 3 4 5 6 7 8 9 10 11 12

Inches
12 9 6 3 0   1   2   3   4   5   6   Feet

96

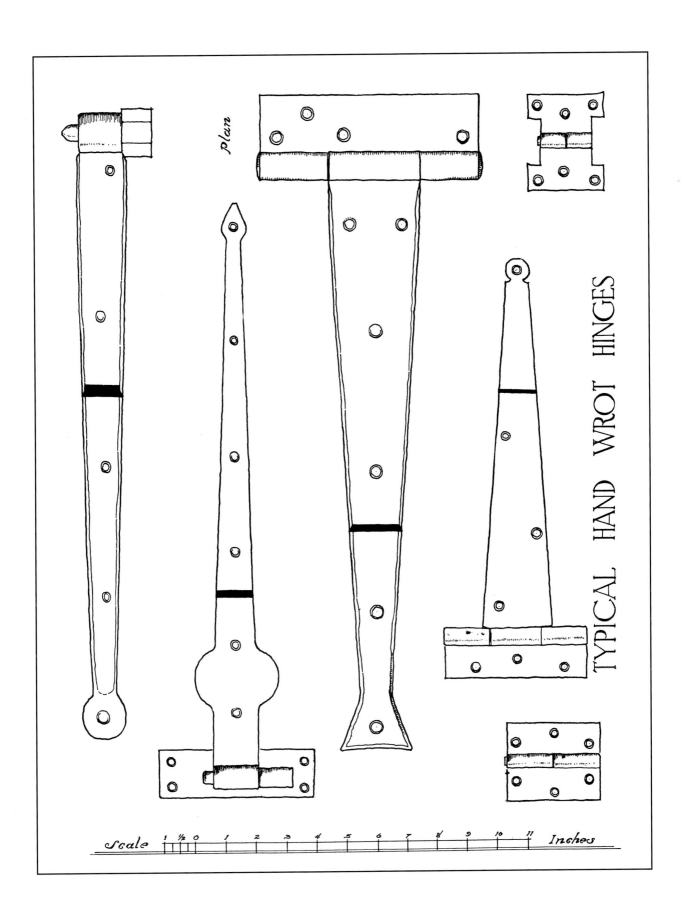

Plan

TYPICAL HAND WROT HINGES

Scale 1 ½ 0 1 2 3 4 5 6 7 8 9 10 11 Inches

97

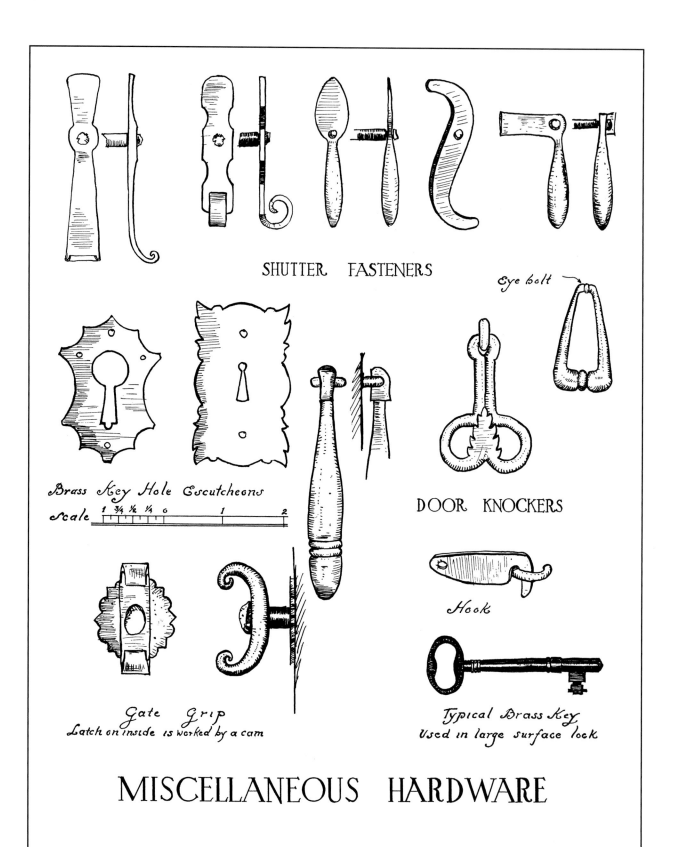

SHUTTER FASTENERS

Eye bolt

Brass Key Hole Escutcheons

Scale

DOOR KNOCKERS

Hook

Gate Grip
Latch on inside is worked by a cam

Typical Brass Key
Used in large surface lock

MISCELLANEOUS HARDWARE

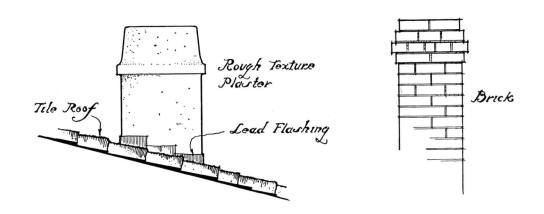

Rough Texture
Plaster

Tile Roof

Lead Flashing

Brick

Chimneys Were Generally Small
And Usually Came thru the Roof
Rather than Being on Exterior.

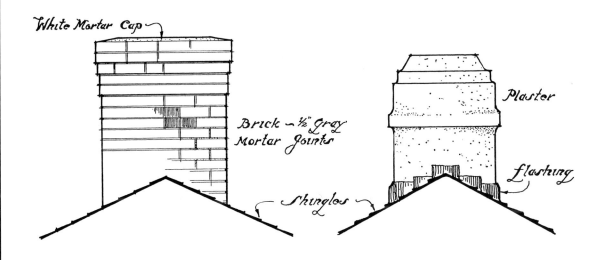

White Mortar Cap

Brick - ½" Gray
Mortar Joints

Plaster

Flashing

Shingles

TYPICAL CHIMNEY TOPS of MONTEREY

Inches 12 9 6 3 0   1   2   3   4   5   6   Feet

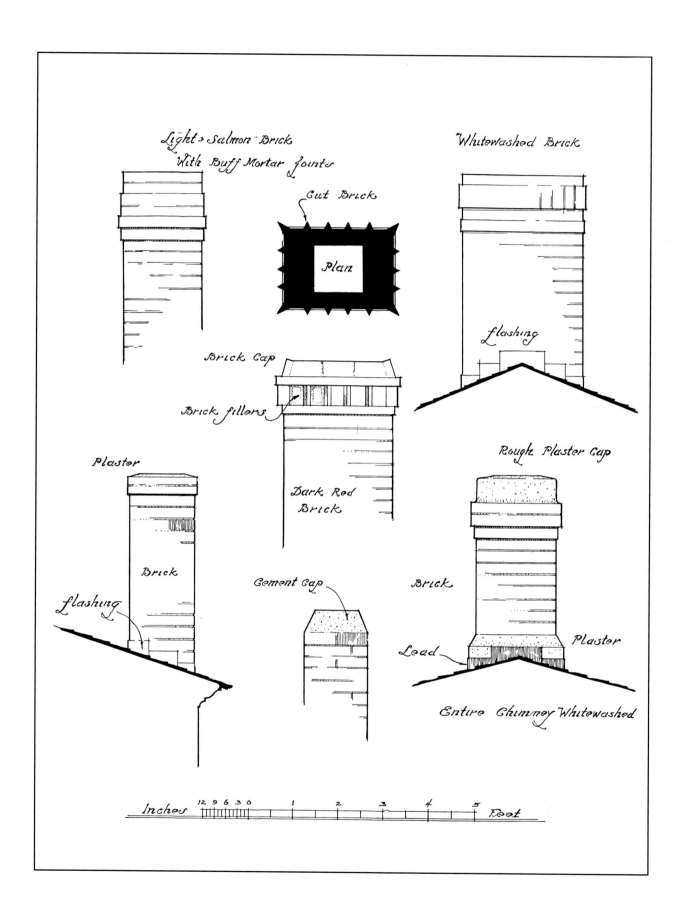

Light & Salmon Brick
With Buff Mortar Joints

Whitewashed Brick

Cut Brick

Plan

Brick Cap

Brick fillers

flashing

Plaster

Dark Red
Brick

Rough Plaster Cap

Brick

Brick

Cement Cap

Lead

Plaster

flashing

Entire Chimney Whitewashed

Inches 12 9 6 3 0   1   2   3   4   5   Feet

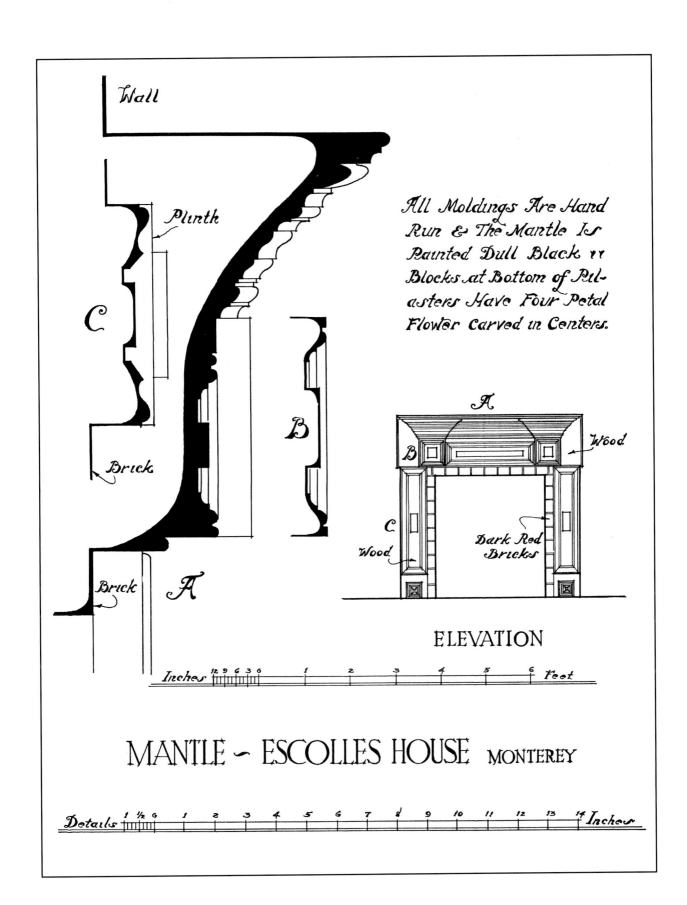

Wall

Plinth

C

Brick

Brick

A

B

All Moldings Are Hand Run & The Mantle Is Painted Dull Black " Blocks at Bottom of Pilasters Have Four Petal Flower Carved in Centers.

A

B

Wood

C

Wood

Dark Red Bricks

ELEVATION

Inches 12 9 6 3 6 1 2 3 4 5 6 Feet

MANTLE - ESCOLLES HOUSE MONTEREY

Details 1 ½ 6 1 2 3 4 5 6 7 8 9 10 11 12 13 14 Inches

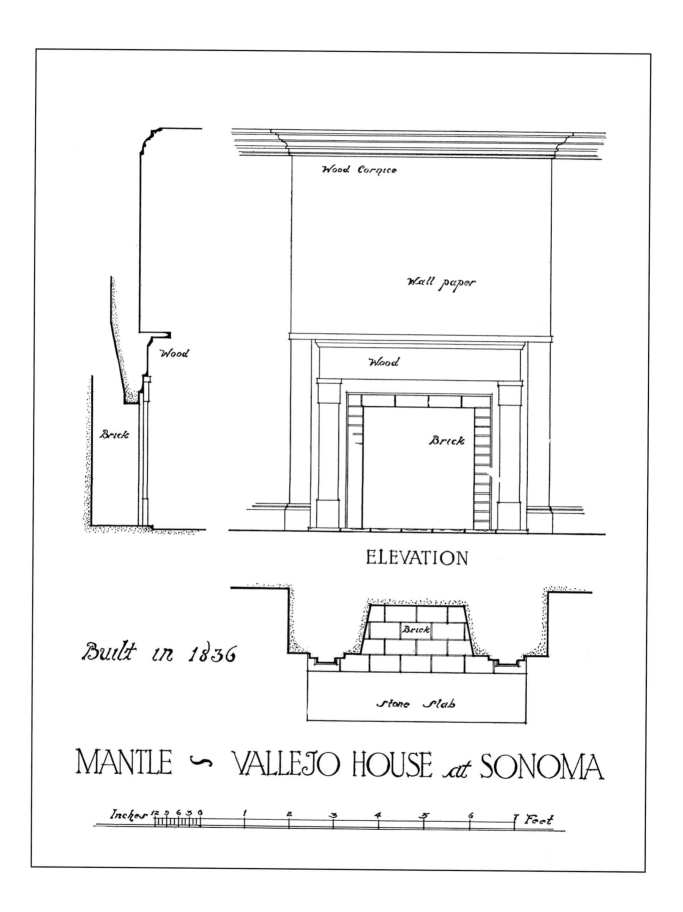

Wood Cornice

Wall paper

Wood

Brick

Wood

Brick

Brick

ELEVATION

Built in 1836

Brick

Stone Slab

MANTLE ∽ VALLEJO HOUSE at SONOMA

Inches 12 9 6 3 0   1   2   3   4   5   6   7 Feet

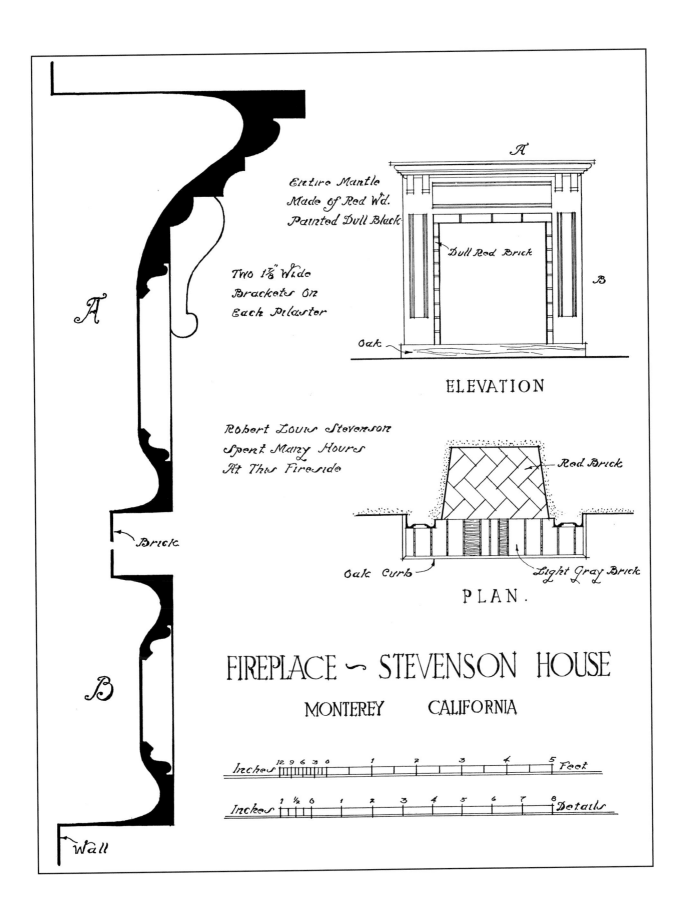

Entire Mantle
Made of Red Wd.
Painted Dull Black

Two 1⅞" Wide
Brackets On
Each Pilaster

A

Dull Red Brick

B

Oak

ELEVATION

Robert Louis Stevenson
Spent Many Hours
At This Fireside

Red Brick

Brick

Oak Curb

Light Gray Brick

PLAN.

B

FIREPLACE ~ STEVENSON HOUSE

MONTEREY   CALIFORNIA

Wall

Inches 12 9 6 3 0   1   2   3   4   5 Feet

Inches 1 ½ 0   1   2   3   4   5   6   7   8 Details

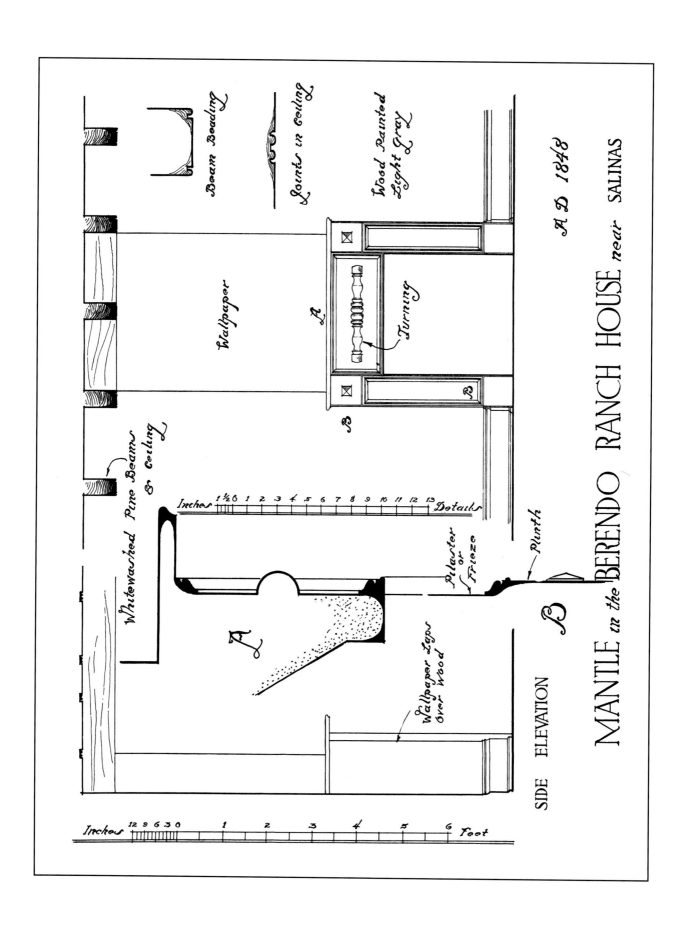

Beam Beading

Joists in Ceiling

Wood Painted Light Gray

A D 1848

MANTLE in the BERENDO RANCH HOUSE near SALINAS

Wallpaper

A

Turning

B

Whitewashed Pine Beams & Ceiling

Inches 1½ 6 1 2 3 4 5 6 7 8 9 10 11 12 13 Details

A

Pilaster or Frieze

Plinth

Wallpaper Laps Over Wood

B

SIDE ELEVATION

Inches 12 9 6 3 0 1 2 3 4 5 6 Feet

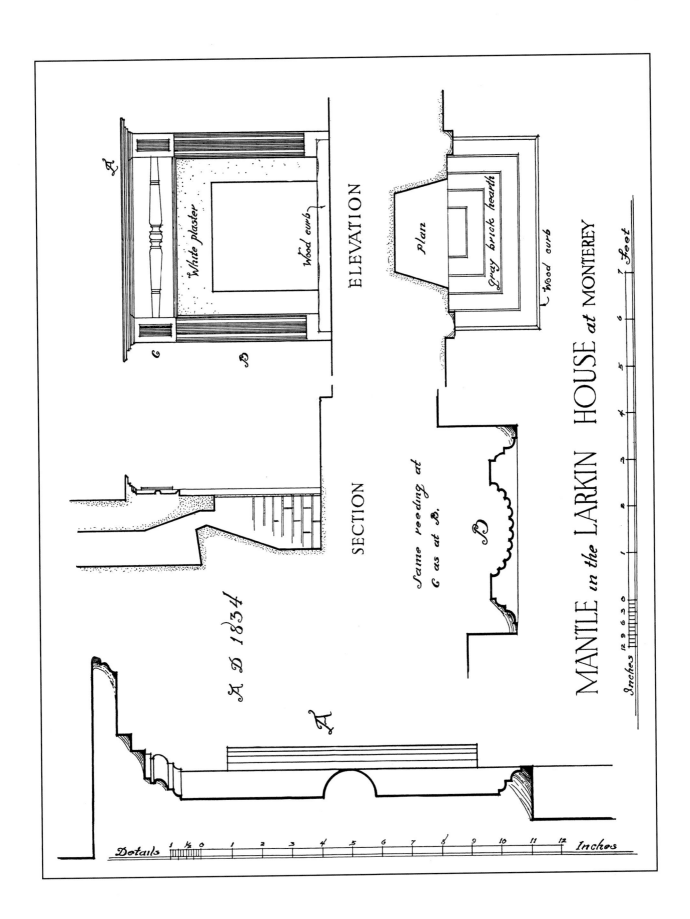

ELEVATION

White plaster

Wood curb

Plan

Gray brick hearth

Wood curb

SECTION

Same reeding at
C as at B.

A D 1834

A

Details

MANTLE *in the* LARKIN HOUSE *at* MONTEREY

Inches

Feet

Door Casing Chair Rail Shutter

Inches ½ 0 1 2 3 4 5 6 7 8 9 10 11 12 13 14 15 Details

Beam

Whitewashed plaster walls~fairly smooth.
Pine ceiling~hewn boards of random widths
from 10" to 16"~& beams painted dull white.
Shutters, sill & trim painted light yellow ochre.
Pine floor wide boards as in ceiling~stain-
ed dark brown. Ceiling height 8'-5"

Base

INTERIOR of the SOBERANES HOUSE at MONTEREY

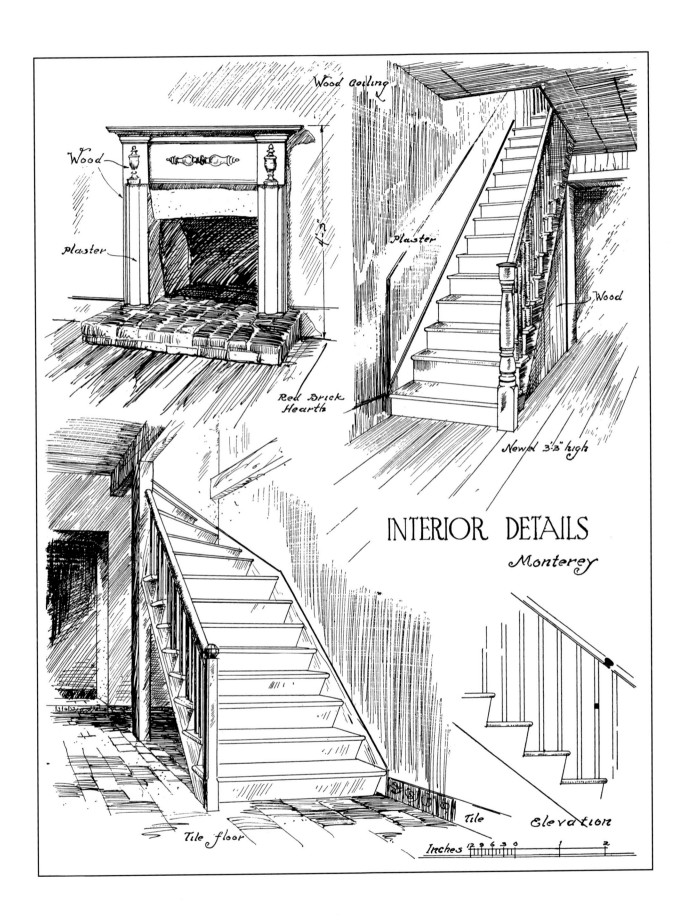

Wood Ceiling

Wood

Plaster

Plaster

Wood

Red Brick Hearth

Newel 3'-3" high

INTERIOR DETAILS

Monterey

Tile floor

Tile

Elevation

Inches

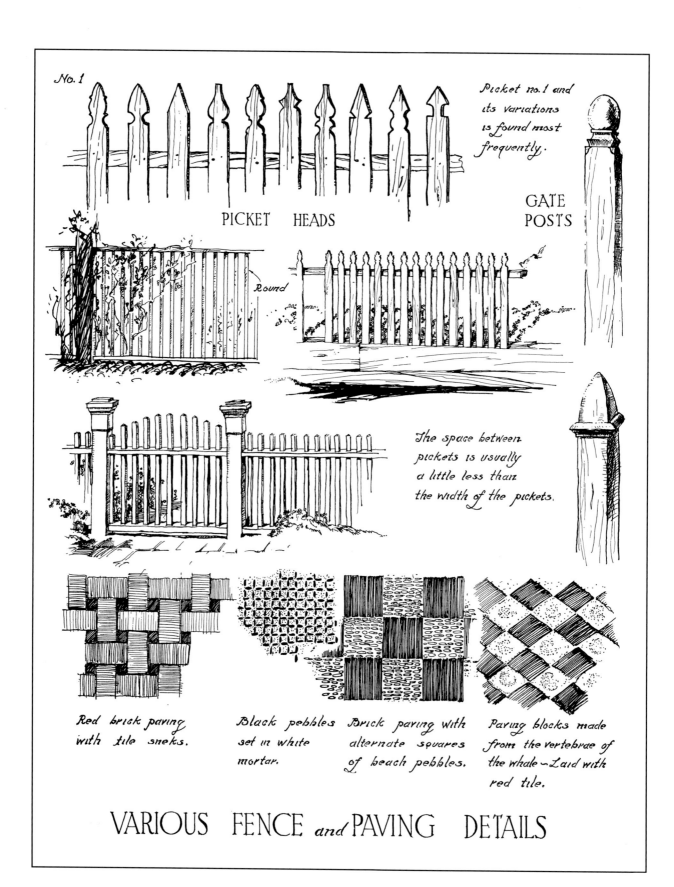

No. 1

PICKET HEADS

Picket no. 1 and its variations is found most frequently.

GATE POSTS

Round

The space between pickets is usually a little less than the width of the pickets.

Red brick paving with tile sneks.

Black pebbles set in white mortar.

Brick paving with alternate squares of beach pebbles.

Paving blocks made from the vertebrae of the whale—Laid with red tile.

VARIOUS FENCE and PAVING DETAILS

Fine cornice
in the Vallejo
house at
Sonoma

Base Molds

Chair Rail

Cornices

Narrow muntins were
a marked characteristic
of nearly all the adobes.
Right muntin used most.

Inch   0 ¼ ½ ¾ 1   Muntins

Wood
Reveal

plaster

Door & Window Casings

TYPICAL MOLDINGS

Scale 1 ½ 0 1 2 3 4 5 6 7 8 9 10 11 Inches

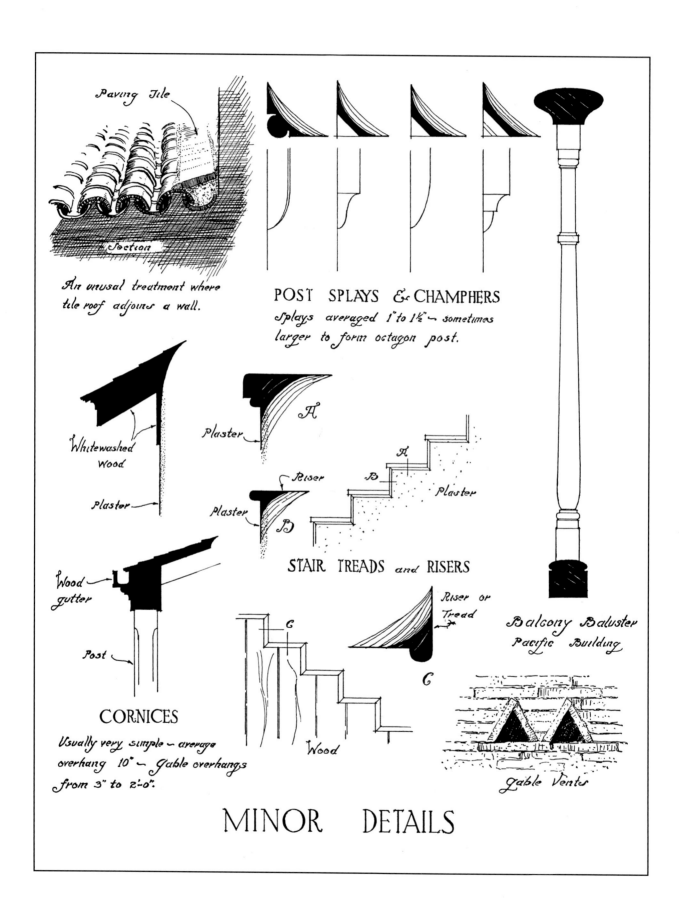

Paving Tile

Section

An unusual treatment where
tile roof adjoins a wall.

POST SPLAYS & CHAMPHERS
Splays averaged 1" to 1½" — sometimes
larger to form octagon post.

Whitewashed
Wood

Plaster

Plaster

Plaster

A

Riser

Plaster

B

A

B

Plaster

STAIR TREADS and RISERS

Wood
gutter

Post

CORNICES
Usually very simple — average
overhang 10" — Gable overhangs
from 3" to 2'-0".

C

Wood

Riser or
Tread

C

Balcony Baluster
Pacific Building

Gable Vents

MINOR   DETAILS